EISENSTEIN 2
A PREMATURE CELEBRATION OF EISENSTEIN'S CENTENARY

IN THE SAME SERIES OF EISENSTEIN TEXTS

SERIES EDITOR: JAY LEYDA

EISENSTEIN
2

A PREMATURE CELEBRATION OF
EISENSTEIN'S CENTENARY

Edited with an Introductory Note by
JAY LEYDA

Translated by
ALAN Y. UPCHURCH, N. LARY,
ZINA VOYNOW, SAMUEL BRODY

A Methuen Paperback

A Methuen Paperback

First published in Great Britain in 1988 by
Methuen London Ltd, 11 New Fetter Lane, London EC4P 4EE
and in the United States of America by
Methuen Inc, 29 West 35th Street, New York, NY 10001,
in association with Seagull Books, Calcutta

ISBN 0 86132 100 6

Printed in India at
Sun Lithographing Company, Calcutta

Cover design by Ashit Paul
with Eisenstein's sketch captioned
'Position at work'

INTRODUCTORY NOTE

No. 2—does that mean there will be a No. 3, 4, . . . ? Yes, we think so—we certainly want so. There is still plenty waiting for translation and waiting for publication. We hope to continue our modest project without interfering with the very large translation plan begun by the British Film Institute: to bring into English the most valuable Russian texts in the original six volumes of Eisenstein's *Writings* that began publication in 1964 on the initiative of his widow, Pera Attasheva.

That leaves a great deal for us. Correspondence, for example, does not figure in the B.F.I. project, and more of his letters come to light constantly. Of his theoretical and critical and autobiographical writing, and working notes, the report from his archive says that bottom has not yet been reached. Although it is risky to make firm announcements for such an improvised series as ours, we see two themes forming themselves into collections. One will probably be entitled 'Disney — Colour — Ivan', and another, on theatre and film, is in the making. Something more urgent may turn up to pre-empt these subjects for the present. Much more waits to tempt Alan Upchurch's translation skill and Seagull's energy.

No. 2 was fun to do, but good things intended for the 'Celebration' now have to wait to be fitted into later numbers. There is no sign of the well drying up. Sergei Mikhailovich was a prolific and tireless worker. He was also his own best archivist, with a sure sense that his work had a future.

Keep in touch with us,
Jay Leyda

CONTENTS

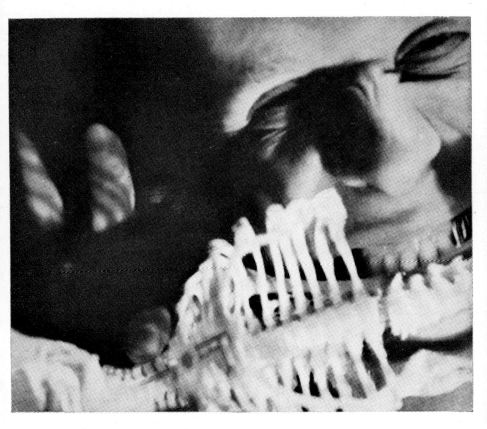

Eisenstein's Unequal Struggle with an Embryo's Skeleton (1934)

Falling Out of Proletkult

In the list of Eisenstein's Published Writings (in Film
Essays) *the description of these pieces of 1925 is not ac-
curate. The first of the three pieces was an interview given by
Eisenstein to* Kino-nedelya *(No. 2) on his departure from
Proletkult, on the completion of* Strike *and on his film plans.
His assistant, Mormonenko, now took the name of Alexandrov. The second piece (in No. 6), an open letter signed
by Valeri Pletnyov, was issued by the directorate of the Proletkult Theatre in defence of its policies. (N. Lary, tran-
slator of the three documents, has made no effort to improve
Pletnyov's crude language.) The third (in No. 10) is
Eisenstein's attempt to end the useless debate. For Pletnyov it
was not the end: he later joined Shumyatsky's staff in a more
terrible assault on the art of Eisenstein.*

Kino-nedelya, No. 4, 1925, p. 7

Interview with the Director S. M. Eisenstein

[Interviewer: A. L-ec]

Strike, a Goskino assignment, is now finished and is passing
through the censorship. *Strike* is my first and last [film] col-
laboration with the first workers' theatre, the Proletkult, for
I left this theatre in the beginning of December. The occasion
for this was a somewhat unseemly matter—the Proletkult
Executive Bureau's failure to recognize my rights as co-author
of the script of *Strike*. My reason for coming out was of course
deeper: over the past year, my work could not conform with
the patently, theatrically (formally) reactionary direction taken
by the ruling circles of the Proletkult, with the passing of
influence to persons who had always opposed what I did and
who stubbornly defended the 'Right' point of view in the

theatre. The slant taken in the work since my departure is evidence of the Proletkult Theatre's complete break with the so-called 'Left camp', so that the camp of our theatrical enemies is now strengthened. This is of course a matter of regret, in the first place for the outstandingly young and healthy collective [of the Theatre], which, after a two-year respite, is back in the ring with successive directors, 'platforms', and so-called searchings, despite the fact that these searchings since 1917 amount to no more than a succession of individual styles and tenets of different theatrical workers.

The break with the Proletkult finally impels me to give my all to film work, for the immediate future at any rate. I have thus turned down the only appropriate proposal—to be a director in the Meyerhold Theatre—in view of the grandiose scope of my new undertaking, a heroic Romantic embodiment of the history of the Horse-Army, an amazing subject for film, and because of my need to travel about the USSR for at least six or seven months.

At present, Comrade Bliokh, ex-Red Army (and Head of Production, Moscow Section, Sevzapkino), and my assistant, Comrade Mormonenko (who left the Proletkult with me), are organizing the historical materials and the oral and written records of participants (Comrade Budyonny, Voroshilov, Kalinin, Beloded, Afanasenko, and others) and, with due despatch, are working out the script, which falls into the following parts—Partisans, Cavalry Division, and the Horse-Army. It will show thematically and historically the manifestation of collective and personal heroism, and the organizing role of the Party, which with iron energy succeeded in forging the Horse-Army mass.

Formally: a development of the ideas expressed by me in *Strike*—themes of the social mass.

The film *Horse-Army* will be 2000–2500 metres long. For the battle scenes—the most difficult task to carry out—military specialists and battle participants are available. We are boldly counting on the participation of the latter, bearing in mind Comrade Kalinin and Voroshilov's wish to have some of the film output of 1928 devoted to the Red Army (in the Fifth anniversary speeches for the Red Army) and since moreover Comrade Voroshilov has agreed along with Comrade Budyonny to collaborate on the realization of this film, which in effect they themselves initiated.

Kino-nedelya, 1925, No. 6, p. 9

An Open Letter to the Editors of the Journal *Kino-nedelya*

Dear Comrades,

In issue No. 4 of your paper, dated the 21st of this month, there appears an interview with S. M. Eisenstein about the Proletkult's picture *Strike* and about S. M. Eisenstein's leaving the Proletkult. There too the Moscow Proletkult ExecBureau is accused of a 'somewhat unseemly matter'—failure to recognize S. M. Eisenstein's rights as co-author of the script of *Strike*.

This is now the second instance of a pronouncement in the press by S. M. Eisenstein to which we must publish a refutation.

In the first place, S. M. Eisenstein did not 'come out' of the Proletkult; he was gone out [*sic*].

Here are the facts: On 4/XII 1924 the ExecBureau considered Eisenstein's claim, in which the latter claimed, 'I worked out the most detailed script' (of the picture *Strike*) and hence asserted full authorship of the script of *Strike*.

The ExecBureau of the Moscow Proletkult brought down this ruling:

'It is found that the suit brought by S. M. Eisenstein for exclusive author's rights (for the *Strike* script) is presumptuous, and the nature and specific tone of his claim inadmissible.'

'It is recognized that S. M. Eisenstein, with his latest pronouncements and with his whole relationship to the Proletkult, has created a situation that precludes his remaining in the Proletkult; hence he is to be released from work in the Proletkult.'

It was only after this ruling, once he had heard about it, that S. M. Eisenstein sought to submit his resignation by telephone, which as an official submission was not accepted over the telephone. The next day his resignation was submitted in writing, when it was no longer necessary, as S. M. Eisenstein had been removed from the list of Proletkult cadres by the ruling of the ExecBureau. Of course it suits S. M. Eisenstein proudly and worthily to claim: 'I came out of the Proletkult.' But this is only 'putting a good face on things'.

It is extremely characteristic of S. M. Eisenstein that in the interview of which we are speaking, he now claims that what was not recognized was *only his co-authorship* of the script of *Strike*.

This right too we did not recognize, do not recognize, and shall not recognize. The script of *Strike* was worked out by a collective of Proletkult workers, with the further participation during the process of evaluation by some Goskino workers, Comrades Ivanov, Goldobin and Shutko, and a series of comrades belonging to the collective of the First WorkTheatre of the Proletkult. In this work S. M. Eisenstein too had a part. Consequently we can recognize his part in the collective work on the script of *Strike*. This no one denied him.

These are the facts that can testify to the 'seemliness' of the behaviour and actions of S. M. Eisenstein.

Regarding the remainder of the interview, we must make these declarations:

The Proletkult ExecBureau had to wage a fierce struggle against his formally 'revolutionary' tendency, expressed in a striving for superfluous, self-directed formalism and gimmickry in working out the director's plan for the film; and against the introduction into the plan of a number of dubious incidents of Freudian purport.

We now have material on the evaluation of the film and its 'revolutionary', formal achievements by the really revolutionary proletariat, to the judgment of which we presented our film. This criticism shows what value is placed on Eisenstein's 'revolutionariness'.

The Proletkult did not deny and does not deny Eisenstein's abilities as a director, but has always waged a fierce struggle against his formalistic and psychoanalytic twistings.

Regarding Eisenstein's 'revolutionariness', and the 'reactionariness' of the ruling circles of the Proletkult, the only possible reply is this: the Proletkult, standing in the left camp of the theatre, never refused and is not now refusing the struggle, inside and out, against narrow formalism, against leftism. To make pronouncements in the cause of leftism concerning the Proletkult's future paths is not up to Eisenstein. The crocodile tears Eisenstein sheds over the Proletkult collective are all the more ridiculous. Eisenstein should remember that among directors he is not 'the unique and incomparable rowanberry liquor of Nezhin' described in advertisements. Only his excessive self-assurance leads him to put himself in what is, seriously speaking, a ridiculous position.

On behalf of the ExecBureau,
Moscow Proletkult,
V. PLETNYOV

Kino-nedelya, 1925, No. 10, p. 22

Letter to the Editor

Comrades!

I ask you to publish these remarks on Comrade Pletnyov's refutations in your paper, issue No. 6, of the interview with me published in issue No. 4.

Not being a master of Comrade Pletnyov's style of writing, I shall keep exclusively to the business side of things. A detailed analysis of the situation and of Comrade Pletnyov's account of the motives for which I was 'gone out', i.e. his account of the *occasion* of my leaving—only indicates that there were more reasons on my side for leaving the Proletkult than there were on the side of the Proletkult to remove me. In truth the motives were my attitude to the Proletkult, and in no way that 'revolutionariness in quotation marks' of my formal achievements which was suddenly brought up when I was setting forth my main reason for leaving—the Moscow Proletkult ExecBureau's reactionariness in theatre matters. Before this my work had evidently been of sufficient ideological relevance for the Proletkult, otherwise why should the Proletkult in the middle of November have concluded an agreement with me for May, on fairly heavy terms for its budget? At this time the ExecBureau could have parted with me without the conflict and even perfectly quietly, say, simply by turning down my terms or on the grounds of my refusal to take part in a certain portion of the overall output plan of the theatre (including two plays by Pletnyov, which I categorically refused to put on in view of their formal and theatrical qualities).

As for the actual fact of my going from the Proletkult, I must announce, unfortunately for Comrade Pletnyov, that it was *definitely* settled not by the ExecBureau ruling dated 4/xii, but instead two weeks earlier, when an initiating group from the collective, knowing my inclination to leave the Proletkult altogether, came to me with a fairly unexpected statement of their intention to leave the Proletkult (for other ideological and organizational considerations). They requested me to take charge of this group out of the WorkTheatre, aiming to set up as a district itinerant company. For this fact, there are— unfortunately—23 living witnesses, headed by the ComUnit of the WorkTheatre. On 5/xii notice was given of the departure from the Theatre of the RCP Unit to be followed in a few days by the remaining comrades. My departure, which had been decided upon and postponed for a while, until in particular the question of my co-authorship of *Strike* should have been cleared up, determined their departure and took place on 4/xii in the somewhat unforeseen form lovingly expounded by Comrade Pletnyov. The only corrections to make are that I asked, over the telephone, whether the ExecBureau—after making its quite unexpected decision of 'nonrecognition'— was going to consider, as a logical consequence, the question of my dismissal, whereupon it was communicated to me through the

Administrative Assistant (Comrade Iazvitskaia) that the question was being considered but was not resolved. After this I sent a telephonogram preempting the decision. As it subsequently emerged, the question had already been decided in principle, and the hold-up was only a formality. Accordingly my notice appeared to be too late; and the ExecBureau, taking for the first time in our joint work the standpoint of orthodox formalism, can 'proudly and worthily' (in Pletnyov's words) write: 'we have gone out Eisenstein.'

Regarding the comrades from the collective, the Proletkult administration used the collective agreement and trade union legislation to annul their mass departure. This I suppose suffices not for 'crocodile tears', but rather for an expression of sympathy for the collective, inasmuch as a group of forcibly detained people does not quite correspond to the concept of a collective. What will remain of it in future will appear in May, upon the expiry of the collective agreement.

My conjectures about the succession of directors have been verified, while the 'running times' are even shorter than I expected. (Thus Comrade Roshal lasted or was able to stand only one month and already has a successor.)

As for the co-authorship of the script of *Strike*, I shall of course not look to the Proletkult for 'recognition'. I will only indicate that I never asserted exclusive authorship of the script, and so Comrade Pletnyov is resorting to demagoguery. My claim to the ExecBureau for the remuneration of authors contained four names: Pletnyov, Eisenstein, Mormonenko and Kravchunovsky (the last two being technical assistants). The reply of Comrade Pletnyov to the ExecBureau's inquiry about this matter contained to my knowledge two persons named in error—the historical expert and the collective's delegate charged with equalizing members' workloads.

The authorship passed to the 'authors' collective' at the time when my 13-point itemization of participation in the script reached the ExecBureau in response to the ExecBureau's inquiry as to what, in actuality, I had done. Until then the 'author' for practical purposes had been Comrade Pletnyov, who bore the 'official mandate' for the script.

I think that such a situation, where 'one man has the plough, and seven have a spoon' (even if there were four of us) must be due to a sad confusion resulting from certain comrades' very strange notions about collective creation (for instance, the inclusion of the Goskino comrades, who must have been extremely surprised by this!) and from a fair lack of ideas about script technique and work in general.

To the political and personal onslaughts I feel I do not need to reply. To the former my reply will be all my future work, and for the latter I leave everything to V. F. Pletnyov's conscience—their passionateness has 'human, all too-human' reverberations.

With comradely greetings,
S. EISENSTEIN

Letters to Japanese Colleagues

Eisenstein's early attraction to Japanese culture, especially its theatre, is well known. It is emphasized in these two letters, the first a fragment of 1928 to the critic and historian, Akira Iwasaki, the second written from Mexico in December 1931 after receiving Mr Kobayashi's book on Kabuki make-up.

I

For ten long years I've yearned to visit your remarkable country.

It was inevitable that on my first steps into the world of theatre I would discover the 'Kabuki' and the 'Noh', that treasure of *real* theatre, and that I would become its ardent admirer. We all are indebted to it for our understanding of theatre.

I am delighted that our two countries come closer together— the two countries that have brought the development of theatre to so high a cultural level.

It makes me extremely happy to find kinship in your views on cinema and in you—a friend.

S. Eisenstein

[translated from a facsimile of the Russian text, by Zina Voynow]

2

II

Eisenstein to Masaru Kobayashi; his English
text is reproduced here without change

[Stationery of Imperial Hotel, Mexico City]

14/XII – 31

Dear Mr. Kobayashi!

I just got your marvellous book on 'Kumadori' and am
absolutely delighted by its contents and charmed by the taste
and fine artistry of the edition as such—another proof of the
profound artistic feeling of the people of your country I love
so very much.

It makes me twice as much regret that 11 years ago I did
not continue to study the Japanese language after working four
months on it! I feel that I loose a lot in not being able to read
the text, which I suppose is even more brilliant than the
pictorial material you so finely gathered togethered.

The thing I would like to see would be to have your book
translated into all european languages and I am quite sure it
would be an enormous success. If you should decide to do it
and would like to have my foreword of introduction of your
book to the occidental spirit and mind, I should be happy and
proud to do it.

Meanwhile I will probably have very soon a whole list of
questions to you concerning details and some of the most
interesting schemes in the text. I want to be precise and will
take some time to pose them correctly to your friendly attention.

Besides all connected with Kabuki, there is another subject
which interest me very much according to the studies I am
undertaking in the actual moment: and that is Japanese
chiromancy—the science of the lines in the hand—which for
me are the hyerogliphics of the expressive movements made
by the hand. I made some very interesting discoveries in this
field in the occidental documents and am very curious to know
about oriental theories and practice in unwinding the lines

RECEIPT FOR REGISTERED ARTICLE

Masaru Katayachi
Takahikawa-cho Fushigu
Kioto

78 Ruination
769 % No. Upton
Pasadena California

To
Kioto

Mr Masaru Katayachi—No, 4
Takahikawa-cho
Tatragramu
Kyoto To

Hotel Imperial

S. L. Bernstein

Dear Mr Katayachi!

I just got your marvelous
book on "humanism" and am
absolutely delighted by my
contents and deemed my
the taste an I fine entirely
the contents an of me
and have a joy of me
of the eternity more of the
of my protest in front of
Many and your feeling of
as and your cannot
am only too add much.
It makes
ago I did
it apt that

If I can
and continued
I will
I hop to be it
of months in me
to Russia and
the pleasure of me
to have a of
the greater need
in front at the
interesting schedule
I want to face
and have some time
correctly No Mon
attention.
Please all carry
when in another situation and then

of the hands into caracter, which is but a degree of the usual and habitual movements and attitudes of men. If you should happen to fall on some material in this line, you would oblige me very much in communicating them to me.

I hope to be in Japan in a couple of months on my way back to Russia—and expect to have the pleasure of meeting you and have a good talk about the Japanese theatre—the matter of my greatest enthusiasm for years and years.

I await your friendly answer; am writing you additional questions and thank you sincerely for your admirable book.

Yours truly
S. Eisenstein

P.S. There is another special question which interests me very much—and that is the question of actors education in Japan (the classical schools).

P.P.S. I shall inform you about my arrival as soon as everything will be fixed, but still you can get all the details about that from mister I. Fukoro, 37 Mamiana [?]—cho, Asabu-Ku, Tokyo, who is taking care of our trip.

On Imagery

These two pieces were first published in Voprosy liter-
atury, *Moscow, in 1968 (see 'Published Writings', No.
312). The first can be tentatively dated 1933; the second is
the transcribed stenogram of a lecture given at GIK, 21
September 1928. In the plan of his book on 'Pushkin and
Cinema' Eisenstein had more to say on Zola and Balzac (see
'Lessons from Literature', in* Film Essays).

I

Whenever the subject of cinema and literature is discussed,
especially with girls, you inevitably hear the question:

'Oh! Why doesn't anyone film Dos Passos,—he's so cinematic . . .'

That, my dear young lady, is precisely the reason no one
films him!

His cinematic quality comes from the cinema. His devices—
are film devices, borrowed, second-hand.

During my war-time student years, I had a certain classmate
by the name of Salnikov.

A member of the Black Hundred and an activist.

Stalwart and eloquent.

'They should print his speeches in "Novoye Vremya",'—
the students would say.

To which others would reasonably reply: 'Not at all. That's
where he took them from . . .'

Such is the fertilizing role for film devices played by 'ultra-
cinematic' writers.

It's the same as trying to reproduce the movement of your
reflection in a mirror . . .

There are writers who write in a way I'd call directly
cinematic.

They see in terms of 'shots'. Or even parts of shots. And they write in terms of montage lists.

Some see in terms of montage lists.

Others describe events.

Still others arrange images cinematically.

In some, we can find all these traits together.

For example, Zola.

Zola sees concretely. He writes in terms of people, windows, shadows, temperatures . . .

A page by Zola could easily be broken down and numbered as a montage list and its sections distributed to the various production departments. Here's a shot composition for the cinematographer. Here are sketches for the Art Director and Wardrobe Designer. Here's the lighting design for the Lighting Cameraman. Here's the *mise-en-scène* for the Director. Here's the montage outline for the Editor. And the sound effects score for the Sound Engineer . . .

Malicious 'Zolaism'?

However much 'Zolaism' makes me grind my teeth, I won't stop recommending and . . . continuing to teach myself the art of employing all five senses. For ascetic judges all suffer a common defect: where Zola's vision is synthesized, theirs is composited. And if the first results in the keenest capacity for differentiation, then the second represents the method of . . . 'indiscrimination'. And this method is characterized by the inability to distinguish what is useful and necessary even alongside something harmful. Nothing is definite by moonlight . . .

But as ill-luck would have it, Engels praised Balzac and spoke less warmly of Zola.

But we should ask: *from what viewpoint?*

La Comédie Humaine provides the most remarkable, realistic history of French society from 1816 to 1848. Even in terms of economic detail, it provides more than all the books by professional historians. Finally, Balzac ingeniously and historically branded the departing social régime and was able to discern and correctly portray those people who were coming to take its place, in spite of the fact that he belonged in his heart to the former.

Try to begin speaking about Zola, and zealous quotations immediately come at you like a sling or catapult.* It's perfectly obvious that for a full-blooded scope of the social phase through the acts of living people, we should turn first to Balzac and not to Zola.

And it's equally clear that the social panorama in living images is of foremost and fundamental importance.

But this is not everything. There still remains the *method* of embodiment. And this is such a crucial 'part' that all the assets of the first can be totally wiped out by the deficits of the second.

And here in terms of the *purely cinematic* use of and grounding in the classics, there arises something unforeseen and unexpected.

Balzac's outline and creation of the social face of the epoch and the physiognomy of the social epoch (images of people) are unsurpassed.

But Balzac's devices of exposition, devices of description, devices of embodiment weaken when it comes to . . . film, and even more so to picture length; that is, to the motion picture's limitations of length.

And the point is not his novels' great length or bulkiness . . .

The chain of descriptive details and the web of subtle features throughout subtle episodes, the canvas of passing ('passage') episodicness, the fabric of the writing itself, all woven into a final, full-blooded relief of the epoch and people, like animal skins around a full-blooded organism,—Balzac's method of *exposition* cannot pass the final test of film—the test of length.

Having already spoken of Flaubert (*Madame Bovary*) and his superior meticulousness of detail and weave of realistic *nuance*, I believe I can now fully outline the prejudice that cinema has against Balzac.

Cinema—is cruder. More commercial, if not necessarily cheaper. It is more like a microscope, where every 'nuance'

* See 'Lessons from Literature', in *Film Essays*.—J.L.

appears as an explosion and the slightest tremble can be rubbed raw and destroy the print of a picture appearing on the distributor's ledgers as forty per cent suitable.

But then suddenly, on the other hand, in comparison to Balzac's assets, Zola's deficits in terms of the scope of images of people or social schematization and rationalization, which often border on oversimplification, turn out to be assets in terms of the *embodiment* of their details and exposition along a cinematic line.

A curious bond, the precursor to that which literature is doing today with cinema, once stamped itself as the most curious contact between literature and painting.

When Gogol joined creative forces with his friend Alexander Ivanov, cinema still wasn't born; and there still was no cinema when this most curious bond no less significantly coupled Zola with Cézanne, Zola with Manet, Zola with the Impressionists.

Impressionism as a *method of cognizance* of concrete reality warrants unconditional condemnation.

But the method of Impressionism, in its laconic transmission of detail, in its reception by the viewer of a sense of unity (if not its philosophical interpretation), proves to be a splendid school for visual film culture.

The luxury of a many-volumed exposition is inaccessible to cinema. Cinema is brought to life by a laconic stroke. By a method of exposition that, combining stroke with stroke, gathers pictures into a final, full-blooded scope.

Laconism, as a means of embodiment in cinema, although mandatory, does not solve everything.

Let's turn not to the Impressionists, but to their teachers—the Japanese.

There is a saying: 'One swallow does not make a spring.'

An underestimation of this sentence would tell disastrously in the work of meteorological stations.

But then a Harunobu or Hokusai, with a single branch of blossoming cherry tree and a vague horizon line with a glimpse of the slope of Mount Fuji, can plunge you into the full fragrance of a Japanese spring.

For a revelation of the inner aspects of Japan, this would be insufficient.

But a laconic stroke is capable of much.

And if the above-mentioned lone swallow does not make a meteorological spring, then we ourselves at least once succeeded in presenting the former, tragic, hungry, 'peasant spring' in three shots of a pregnant woman, an emaciated cow, and a pathetic, protruding branch (*Old and New*).

Here we should include the pince-nez and cord hanging from the hawser in *Potemkin*.

The laconism of an expressive image of a detail, an object, a person.

The laconism of foreshortening, the art of *pars pro toto*—that's what allows even the 'villain' Zola to argue with the Japanese.

And that's what the filmmaker must never cease learning from the novelist.

Laconism is not sketchiness.

In general. And certainly not in this aspect, in Zola's works.

Although that which sparkles in Zola's embodiment with the art of *pars pro toto*, when extended to the personalities of his characters and particularly his depiction of the correlation of social forces—turns into sketchiness.

But Balzac stands at an opposite pole—his unsurpassed sculpture of images of an epoch turn into writing of a type that does not break down into shots and will not take off.

So why don't we study Balzac for the one and Zola for the other?

Oranges and fir-cones grow on different trees.

And when you need some carrots, you don't go looking for them on an orange tree or magnolia . . .

The same is true from the point of view of Zola's usefulness to the specifics of visual embodiment in cinema—Zola, after all, was never condemned by Engels . . .

Laconism through laconism. But it knows a yet higher form of manifestation.

That is when it occurs simultaneously in an image and the whole register of literary forms.

Then you won't be able to reduce a page directly into shooting plans and the changing of shots.

Then it's 'technically' more complicated, but juicier, perhaps even richer.

Then it's a matter of a creative equivalent.

Of a visual image, equivalent to the one not visually noted by the author.

I'm categorically opposed to depending on the author for a visual image.

Speech, sound, graphics, acoustics.

But leave me taste and smell.

Just an image. And the more accessible the realm is to the writer and the more intense the resulting image, the better.

Sometimes the arrangement of words in lines is more valuable to us than a volume filled with graphic images.

When filming Babel, for example, or staging him in the theatre, the most important thing is to reproduce the arrangement of his words through *mise-en-scène*. And above all their texture.

For cinema, these are the keys to montage and shot composition.

It's not the visual worksheets of the writer's image that we need.

What's important for us is the image of the author's thinking and the imagery of his thought.

That's what's most important.

And finally, if you aren't able to see imagery in terms of your own field and its capabilities, then it's pointless to go into filmmaking as a Director.

Somewhere, a long time ago, I wrote that the conception behind the whole 'Drama on the Deck' episode in *Potemkin* grew from a line in someone's recollections: '... in the air there hung a deadly silence', following the summons for the tarpaulin.

There were no nails to hang it with. And the silence did not die. But this extremely modest and visually expressive line was capable of being transposed into a sufficiently persuasive equivalent of a collection of details and actions from naval practice.

Let's not forget the Dnieper River in Dovzhenko's *Ivan*. I believe it to be in full harmony with the exposition of the Dnieper by Gogol. And I'm not talking here about a 'translation'.

And yet it would make a fascinating theme to trace how the twists of structure and melodics of Gogol's writing flow into the refined images of Dovzhenko's shots, alternating with the drowsiness of the camera gliding along the waters, or quickly panning along the winding shore. 'It neither ripples, nor roars', 'Stare into it, and you can't tell whether it moves or not . . .'

Everything is observed and harmoniously caught by the camera so that it blends with Gogol's opening: 'The Dnieper is magical when it's quiet and calm . . .'

Dovzhenko's Dnieper is not a photograph.

Dovzhenko's Dnieper is the most remarkable 'lyrical digression' known to the textbooks of literature and a moving hymn, enrapturing us with the river, with the poet who sings it, and henceforth with the Director who shot it.

Imagery.

The leaping, stone lion in *Potemkin* found it in a place where, till that time, montage had gone no further than parallelism of actions, sometimes approaching visual unity.

The slaughter-house and 'slaughter' in *Strike* is perhaps the harshest and most unrestrained example, but one which established itself as a tradition in our cinema no less than the lions.

The lions of *Potemkin*. If less purebred mothers have inflicted no few imitative mongrels on cinema, then that guilt does not rest with their long-maned parents.

In any event, the disruptions of persuasiveness of visual representation in cinema, I repeat, are also dictated by the very same thing as in literature. To cross over to poetic and visual

language from matter-of-fact writing without a proper grasp or
sufficient emotion is entirely the same absurdity for a writer
in the way it sounds as it is for us.

Whether it's a turn of phrase. Or a twist of plot.

Without the Odessa Steps, the roused lions would be an
absurdity.

At the height of the novel *Nana,* you can't help generalizing
the stupendous scene of the horserace where the mare 'Nana'
triumphs, into the triumph over Paris by Nana, the woman.
A scene possible only as the highest point of a culmination of
real piling up and tension of emotions throughout the chapters
of the novel towards this page.

How pathetically and feebly the finale of the first volume
of *Son Excellence Eugène Rougon* plunges into a far-fetched,
simplistic parallelism, not at the height of pathos gathering
momentum from afar, but 'cold-bloodedly' and artificially
written out as equations with no common unknown quantity:
after the court hunt of Napoleon III, the dog pack racing by
torchlight to tear to pieces the deer . . . And the pack of just
as infernal and hungry adventurers of the court cabal, snatch-
ing at the pieces . . .

And cinema knows precisely the same thing.

The battle-front and the struggle at the Stock Exchange in
Pudovkin's *End of St. Petersburg* merge into a poetic generaliza-
tion from a simple, temporal concurrence.

But the spatial concurrence of the demonstrating marchers
and the ice-drifts in *Mother* does not reach these heights with
its half-baked structure, emotional inappropriateness and lack
of expressive need.

I'm involuntarily reminded here of 'came the rain and two
students'.

Inkizhinov and his horsemen from *The Heir to Jenghis-Khan*
(*Storm Over Asia*) have difficulty in jumping over the barrier
that separates the horses and speeding hooves from the whirl-
wind that sweeps away everything in its path. But Dovzhenko's
horses in *Arsenal* surmount the barrier from horse to generaliza-
tion with ease.

However, the naked peasant woman in *Earth* didn't manage the same pirouette to the heights of 'pantheism' (where they love to place Dovzhenko); she remained earthbound and mundanely inserted into a serious scene of the funeral, and thus came to be considered an obscene element.

As in *October*, our Menshevik haranguing in one shot and harps—in another. Laboriously, laboriously and speculatively, forcibly reduced to an image of 'the heavenly hymns of the Mensheviks at the Second Congress of Soviets'.

Recalling elsewhere in another picture* the *removed* 'hat business' in an image of a top hat with the 'business' papers stuck in it.

I believe this range of examples, from achievements to defeats, outlines in sufficient relief what the point is here.

[1933]

II

An Assignment

I

I'd like to propose the following assignment. One of the greatest masters in 'switching' various concepts is Zola. He possesses an amazing ability to 'switch' any abstract situation, abstract concept over to concrete, real material. But since not all his novels are of equal interest, I have chosen twelve of them and will ask you to pair off and for each person to study one of Zola's novels. First I'd like to analyse, for example, such things as a love situation, a first meeting or first love. This kind of incident occurs in almost all of Zola's novels. All Zola's novels are constructed on the same basis, each exhausting one kind of material. *La Fortune des Rougons* exhausts the setting of a provincial town. *La Faute de l'Abbé Mouret* is constructed on a huge, deserted park. *Le Ventre de Paris* is constructed on one central

* We believe that E's reference is to *Shinel* (The Cloak, 1926), Yuri Tinyanov's script based on two stories by Gogol, directed by Grigori Kozintsev and Leonid Trauberg.

market. *Au Bonheur des Dames*—on a department store; *La Bête Humaine*—on railroads etc. All of Zola's novels can be broken up on this basis. He completely exhausts in one novel some definite material. Given the great length of his novels, there are undoubtedly coinciding situations in each one. It will be interesting to have you dismantle each novel and determine how, let's say, the elements of a first love are materialized here or there. For example, an atmosphere of sensuality, how it is inserted in each material; in *La Terre*, it occurs in conditions of harvesting: in the terrible heat, in the tempo of people reaping, machines, animals and dust. All these elements are placed at the service of a single, sensual, erotic task. In *La Fortune des Rougons*, the conditions for the arousal of a sensual atmosphere are set by the young hero and heroine meeting at night in a cemetery. These heavy vapours of the cemetery, this setting of decay, gradually result in an erotic atmosphere. In *L'Assommoir*, the setting in which these relations develop is a laundry filled with hot steam, heavy air and the smell of washed and unwashed linen. Here there also occurs one of the necessary conflicts. If we take *Le Ventre de Paris*, there the setting for the novel was the basement of a colossal Parisian market. An arched, stone corridor. And at the spot where fowl are slaughtered and plucked, on a mound of feathers, we watch an attempted rape. If we take *La Terre*, the setting will be the storehouses of bread, sacks of flour, and so forth. In *Germinal*, the heroine in the pink peignoir on the coal pile in the depot. In *La Faute de l'Abbé Mouret*, the intoxicating setting that creates a sensual atmosphere is the neglected garden with the long stems and unusual scents. In a word, in each of these novels, the theme of love and its elaboration is attached to some definite material. By analysing in this way how the same situation is elaborated in a different material, we can gather a great reserve of experience in how to materialize a given condition in this or that material. For example, when we came to shoot the Odessa Steps sequence, there arose the question of the firing squad. Here upon the boulevard elements it was necessary to reveal the moment of horror in the execution. In one of the first versions, one of the shocking moments was a killing among baskets of flowers on sale. The execution was to take place among baskets of prickly, dying flowers that live for only one day. They had to express this horror and its individual, psychological moment. In *Potemkin*, they were constructed upon mourning possibilities, drawn from the natural elements of a harbour. And it's Zola's extreme precision of observation and technical achievement that teaches how these things are translated into any given, particular material. I ask you to do the following with each novel: to analyse the material on which the given novel is constructed, determine the scope of the material taken, and identify the most outstanding elements in the realization of this material. For example, in *La Bête Humaine*, there are absolutely remarkable descriptions of the houses near the station and along the railroad. These unique houses, rattling from the motion of the trains, completely and eternally in smoke, the eternal, restless noise of the trains, whistles, etc. In *L'Assommoir*, there is the house with the cheap apartments, the house with separate rooms, the house with a system of corridors, whose characterization is absolutely remarkable: the three streaks of colour which flow from the entrance (somewhere inside this house there is a dye-works). And at different stages of the development of the action, these streaks change colour.

2

FIRST ASSIGNMENT. *Establish the material upon which the thing is constructed, note the outstanding places in presenting this material and by what means this material is displayed.*

This is a question of a purely statistical nature. On what basis, upon what underlying materials is the particular novel constructed? This is simply a catalogue, so to speak.

This question will contain a request of this type: on material of provincial, factory or peasant life, trace through to what extent the whole novel is constructed not only on one type of material, but how it grows in parallel lines. For example, in

Au Bonheur des Dames, there is the parallelism of a large store next to a secondary one. Then in *L'Assommoir*, there is the laundry, the house with the cheap apartments, the one with the various rooms, etc.—here two materials make up this parallelism. It's precisely these knots, these complexes of material that should be explained. If there are several of them, then trace their relations to each other, which of them prevail and in what interrelations and combinations they are given. For example, analyse why and how the boudoir is presented in *L'Assommoir*. Does it have some kind of contrasting relationship to the scene in the laundry or not?

Whoever analyses *La Terre*, it will be interesting to touch upon the question (perhaps a bit off the subject) of how this union was understood in Zola's time! Here there is an extremely curious exposition of the point of view on the interrelations of the peasantry and the workers, despite the fact that the circumstances given here of their union can be excluded, of course, as absolutely inconceivable. It suggests that these two forces must devour each other, and it is on this, apparently, that the novel concludes.

Here our task is to explain to what degree the city is placed in parallel or opposition to the countryside. How do we do this and how is this question resolved there?

SECOND ASSIGNMENT. *The uniqueness of the situations that flow out of the given material.*

Question from class: Could you elaborate on the difference between complexes of material and of situations?

Eisenstein: For example, in *La Bête Humaine*, the scene of the train running into the cart carrying granite is an example of how material that is specific to trains is used for the creation of such a situation. This is a crude example. In *Nana* there are much more refined situations which are born from the fact that precisely this material is taken.

In *Au Bonheur des Dames*, there is a characteristic example, consisting of a discussion about shoplifting in a large store where ladies are caught stealing lace by winding it around themselves. This too is a situation which arises precisely in these conditions.

When you receive material for a script, it's extremely important to find a situation, specific for this or that place, for the given material. Don't graft some neutral adultery onto it, but try to deepen this material by 'eavesdropping' and extracting those possibilities which are its peculiarities.

Question from class: In *Le Ventre de Paris*, would an example of the uniqueness of situation arising from the given material be the scene of the starving man who comes upon a market where there are many delicious things which he can't have?

Eisenstein: Yes. And there it's also necessary to note who nourishes whom in this case. Is this man brought into the market scene for the purpose of displaying the richness and bounty of the market, or the opposite combination? It's interesting to analyse which way the scale tips. Is this person necessary? Is this situation necessary? Or is it a means of revealing this market through a person?

This brings us up against the particular device of presentation. A presentation through some person of the setting you need, or through the setting itself? For Zola tips the scales precisely in this direction—through a portion of reality.

It's important for us to analyse when he introduces a subsidiary element of the subject, in order to present the material with greater persuasiveness. In *Nana*, for example, the action begins in a theatre. I believe that the entire theatre is shown for the sole purpose of presenting this girl at its summit.

Recall the description of the first performance; the theatre loge and so forth are given so as to convey the figure of Nana in greater relief, for she herself plays the same role of basic material as the market does in *Le Ventre de Paris*. Nana is given the same degree of close-up as the market. Material found in other novels is less rich in incidental display.

You should note, for example, how the theatre works in revealing the figure of Nana in the beginning. This concerns those who will be dealing with this novel, and you should contrast your analysis with those of your comrades who are working on *Le Ventre de Paris*.

THIRD ASSIGNMENT. *Note how eroticism is realized in the given material.*

Question from class: I'm reading *La Débâcle*. Either the woman there is presented so subtly that it's difficult to get a sense of her, or I have the impression that the soldiers are so exhausted and so hungry that they feel no relationship of any kind with women?

Eisenstein: In *La Débâcle*, this is the specific or, if you will, erotic sensuality in the conditions of an army setting. In *La Faute de l'Abbé Mouret*, it's the opposite: man in the sun, in a stifling, heady garden from day to day. That's a completely different atmosphere and his is a completely different condition. The very same theme, but with a characteristic contrast, for in the end, Mouret lives exlusively through elements of eroticism, because of the setting in which he is placed.

Question from class: So we're interested not in how Zola gives the erotic parts in terms of literary description and images, but in terms of how he materializes this situation?

Eisenstein: Of course. The most important thing is what gives rise to the culminating moment of sensuality, when it concerns the erotic scenes. What creates the tension of this scene? What details give this feeling? How does he treat them?

Question from class: The question concerns only the details?

Eisenstein: Well, for example, this sort of thing. Take Pudovkin's scene [in *Mother*] of the dripping tap. There you have, as they say, a moment of realization of mood, which in this case is found within a room. He has water dripping, and he limits it to this; but take the harvesting scene in Zola's *La Terre*, when the guy throws himself on the girl. How does he lead up to this moment, how does he accumulate the details from the description of the heat, the labour of the machines, the workers and so forth? How is this then translated into the moment of heightened eroticism? Whoever is reading *L'Assommoir* knows that the atmosphere of the laundry, the warm air

3

and dirty linen are the details that (like the warm down in the cellars in *Le Ventre de Paris*) create the atmosphere of the situation. It's extremely interesting how and when the writer uses this material, and it's particularly in the erotic scenes that these devices are most emphasized. He constantly uses these things, and in the most powerful scenes they stand out in high relief and detail. For example, in *La Bête Humaine*, there is a certain eroticism. There the throat and back of the head are given in close-up, which gives an animal feeling.

Such close-ups continue throughout the entire novel. This is something that stays fixed forever in one's memory.

FOURTH ASSIGNMENT. *The way animal scents are conveyed, which is characteristic of all Zola's novels.*

I'd like to make a small suggestion in reference to *L'Oeuvre*. I'd turn my attention to the figure of the woman, through whom he writes, and the thin figure of the starving child. These should be placed next to each other, as two very curious materials.

Later, there's also the sculptor's studio: the cold clay, the strong smell, the humidity, the shavings. All this is given very correctly.

This assignment should encompass questions of exposition in general, not just in this theme, but throughout the separate sections. For example, the symphony of cheese aromas. This includes the registration in close-up of the impressions created.

FIFTH ASSIGNMENT. *How is the atmosphere of this or that location created?*

This is an assignment that borders closely on the preceding one. You don't necessarily have to separate them.

SIXTH ASSIGNMENT. *How are the complex, ecstatic structures done? That is, identify the places of greatest pathos (the translation of each material into a pathetic exposition).*

You should trace how the material proceeds from the purely naturalistic, matter-of-fact, topographical exposition, with which Zola always begins. How does he start the parting of the waters and arrive at the ocean of linen in the store and the ocean of filth that flows out onto the earth as fertilizer?

SEVENTH ASSIGNMENT. *Identify the most emphasized details—that is, the close-ups.*

What is interesting here is the use of repeated close-ups. Such as the recurrence of the throat in *La Bête Humaine*. In another novel, for example in *L'Assommoir*, it's the streak of paint, now black, now red, now blue. This is a repetition, the ticking of Fate's clock, like Griffith's 'cradle of the ages' [in *Intolerance*]. Or simply a group of special close-ups of an unusual nature, when we could simply say that Zola suddenly shoots a close-up from an unexpected angle.

EIGHTH ASSIGNMENT. *The tempo constructions capable of being transposed into a pure montage list.*

In many cases, Zola's construction is of a purely temporal nature, although for temporal construction it's better to take detective novels. In *Nana*, for example, there is the horserace. There are other moments too, for example: detaining, comparison, compression. How is this material constructed, how is it given in these cases?

NINTH ASSIGNMENT. *What devices are used to sketch the personality of the characters?*

By this question should be understood how personality is revealed: through things, through actions, through setting. What are Zola's devices in general for portraying characters? For example, in Griffith's *Intolerance*, the leader of the 'musketeers' is first shown once, and then the setting of his room is given: pictures of a pornographic nature and various images of nude women. A single pan of his room, combined with his outer mask, is enough to issue him a passport to social undesirability. Zola has two opposite ways of portraying characters. We need to trace how this is done. He has these two ways, but doesn't he have still other devices of characterization? Aren't there other ways? . . .

[21 September 1928]

Letters to a Latin-American Poet

Victoria Ocampo published these four notes from Eisenstein in her Argentine journal, Sur, *in 1974. They were noticed and copied by Anthology Film Archives, through whose courtesy they are published here in a translation by Samuel Brody.*

[Stationery of Imperial Hotel, Paseo de la Reforma, Mexico, D.F.]*

Dear friend!

It is so hot that I am dissolving in a stream of sweat . . . I am now on a thin stretch of land called the Isthmus of Tehuantepec between the Gulf of Mexico and the Pacific. If, descending towards us (geographically—morally would mean rising to the heavens!), the heat *increases*—hell must be a *frigidaire* compared to Buenos Aires!

Anyhow I am enormously flattered by your invitation to contribute to your journal, but . . . I fear that that will be the only result of this invitation—it is impossible to write in a temperature in which one is dying even while doing nothing, *To say nothing about shooting for hours at marvellously feminine dark-coloured girls!*

In any case I shall try to do what I can with what remains of my strength after the daily struggle against the heat!

It would be very kind of you to answer this letter and initiate something like a regular correspondence!

Tehuantepec   Ever very sincerely yours
19 Feb 1931   S. M. Eisenstein
(the address is Hotel Imperial, M.D.F.)

* Note by S.B.: *The italicized words were written in English by S.M.E.*

My address is Mexico D.F.
c/o American Embassy
S. M. Eisenstein

6 August 1931

Very dear friend!

Roberto Montenegro tells me that in spite of all your journal-
istic and editorial activity you have retained some small
memory of myself. This makes me most happy and I promptly
send you a small selection of photos from the film we are
making here. They sketchily represent four of the aspects from
which I see Mexico. (The film evolves slowly and there are
eight!) Tehuantepec, tropical and languid, the trenchant
aridity of central Mexico, the baroque in the pure Spanish
tradition (bull-fights etc.) and the monumental austerity of
Yucatan. The film consists of 7–8 independent episodes located
in different regions, forming a collection of short stories (a
Mexican Boccaccio but not indecent).

I hope you will like them and that you will honour them with
an appearance in your journal. (Many—most of them—are
unpublished, for we have not yet begun the publicity.)

I also hope to hear from you as soon as you receive my letter.

Accept my sincere and respectful affection as well as my
compliments to 'Sur', of which I have had the pleasure to see
the first two numbers.

As ever
S. M. Eisenstein

The captions should include the names:
Direction: S. M. Eisenstein and G. Alexandrov
Cameraman: Tisse.

Very dear friend!

I was delighted to receive your trans-Atlantic postcard and
even more to learn of your intention to visit Moscow. Malraux
and Ehrenburg are now here and it is good for all foreigners

to come and see our extraordinary country. We have no wild blacks ['fauves noirs']—but there are other things that are perhaps remarkable. My entire Mexican adventure ended in the worst possible disaster, as you probably know. The photography (that is very beautiful) is all that remains—but the whole composition, montage etc. is completely destroyed by the imbeciles who managed it. As well as the total epic conception. I so loved Mexico and it is so painful not to be able to express it in this film that's now destroyed ... I hope you will be able to discern where Eisenstein ends and Hollywood idiocy begins! This whole affair so broke my heart that I became disgusted with cinema and have not made another film. Instead I've worked on a big theoretical opus which will be finished in a month. In part it is the lectures and lessons I gave at the Moscow Cinema University. This fall, for the sake of change, I will probably stage a theatre production, returning to films only in January/February 1936. I hope that by then my heart will be hidden by ... scars!

I would very much like to see you in Moscow—a trip across our country should prove very interesting for you.

I await your news and remain ever very affectionately yours.

Cordialement

1 July 34

I am impatient to hear your news! How is 'SUR' doing?

[October 1940]

Very dear Madame!

I was delighted by your telegram and that you liked my 'Alexander Nevsky'.

I would be most happy to resume our correspondence.

Does 'Sur' still exist? And how is it doing?

I should like very much to see some numbers.

I have just finished staging Wagner's 'Walküre' at Moscow's Bolshoi Theatre.

If you wish, I can send you an article and photos as well as all the details that might interest you regarding our cinema and theatre.

Always happy to hear your news

> I remain very sincerely
> yours always
> S. M. Eisenstein

My address:

    USSR Moscow Bolshaya Gruzinskaya 17
        Society for Cultural Relations
          for S. M. Eisenstein

Correspondence with a Friend

Eisenstein's friendship with Esther Shub began with his recognition of her experimental editing principles in fictional films and in her original compilations of archive footage. He was her apprentice on a condensation of the two parts of Fritz Lang's Dr Mabuse, *and she assisted him with the shooting-script of* Strike.

The surviving correspondence begins during the vacation taken by Eisenstein and Alexandrov (Grisha) while filming the General Line (Old and New). *The discussion of the acted film* vs *the unacted (or 'documentary') film is a continuing theme in the correspondence. The citizens of Gagra and other vacationers are unaware of this problem: they enjoy German films with Harry Piel, and buy picture-postcards of a popular actor/manager and a director of various spectacles, including the circus. The latter may be the 'great navigator' of Shub's girlhood.*

Eisenstein's second letter was written during the shooting on the 'Giant' State Farm for the revised ending of Old and New.

E to S   15 May 1928
                                                                   Gagra

My dear friend Esther Ilini . . . but *no no no* (this despicable typewriter doesn't have an exclamation point, and here there should be a minimum of a hundred and fifty)

no no no

I've completely forgotten whom I'm writing to. The *unacteds* are here, the *documentors* and there's no room for childish pathos in letters to them . . . Not a word about feelings, and my letter

Esther Shub

is only a *documentation* . . . Not even a letter, but
   an Abkhazian document . . .
and now that constructivism is also 'out of fashion', let this be
preparations, as our friend the 'Hamburg Accountant' says—
preparations towards an Abkhazian document. In any case, as he
himself puts it, 'letters not about love' strikes me as the most
lyrical and touching thing I've read.*

   So . . . —but typos gain the upper hand, temperament
imperiously demands its own, and to hell with the industrializa-
tion of the handwritten letter—I'll write the rest by hand, but
in a strictly, strictly, strictly documentary fashion (as they
would pronounce it here if the happy Abkhazian people
suspected anything in this—here the playacting Harry Piel
indivisibly holds sway . . .).

   But first of all I want to be guaranteed that you will write me.
Only don't mail it—deliver it in person (and save money on
stamps!) to make sure it gets to me without fail. I *treasure* them.
Because I want to have printed, documented evidence on
paper of your true opinion of me. For it's beginning to seem to
me from time to time that if I were to die, you and the others
would not don mourning mittens and crêpe, but would dress,
in glorification of the unacted,—in wedding attire.

   And so, the documentation begins.

   Year: 1928.

   Month: May.

   Place: Gagra.

We arrived not at all in the typical fashion, having tasted a
preliminary portion of hostility in Tuapsa. Just imagine, all
the mountains are covered with clouds, then from all the
kiosks, postcards of Lyubimov-Lansky stare at you, smugly
'humming' from all the kiosk windows. Luckily, they are
'interrupted' from time to time by long shots (to the knees)
of Williams Trutstsa. We're buying postcards of the great
navigator—to send you this object of your girlhood dreams.

   What a terrible inclination to the routine in the whole health

* The references are to Berlin-published books by Victor Shklovsky, *The Hamburg
Account* (1928) and *ZOO: Letters Not About Love* (1924).

resort—it's even repulsive to write. Children, of course: Adochka, Nelli, Galya, Natella, Yurick, etc. There's a bit of diversity in the name of the boy 'Givi' (most likely not of Christian heritage), which for days on end a number of Armenian women have been shrieking from the top floor. The boy is very young, but judging by the shrillness of the cries directed towards him, is not devoid of initiative.

Naturally there's a 'soul of society'. Naturally—an Engineer. During the day he plays catch with the children. In the evenings—with their mothers. At night he sees to it that the mothers will have more children in the future. Also—catch! There is, of course, a couple who came to Gagra solely with that aim. There's a belief that the beauties of the terrain where the child is conceived will determine his good looks. Remember what Gogol wrote: 'When Mommy was with child—in comes a ram a-bleating', and the child (later, it seems, the chairman of the Povetovoy Court) has the bottom half of a sheep's face. Therefore they avoid mingling with the buffaloes and mostly feast their eyes from the wharf on the panoramas of Gagra, even peering through the viewer of a camera. I don't think they shoot anything. But their affair isn't very important. She's a bit sarcastic. He's too preoccupied. For these reasons, he spends the day at the 'shooting gallery'. She watches. According to Freud, this is, in my opinion, an explicit indication of a sad state of . . . the home. Meanwhile the plywood walls of the shooting gallery are shot up from all directions. Yesterday they repainted them cobalt blue. But the holes weren't painted over . . . And she's just as sarcastic as ever.

Naturally there's also 'a cultured young man'. Alas! You know, intellectual beauty—is always to the detriment of the physical . . . And he's very intellectual. Third floor, no. 42. Here's a cliché of the highest sort. He knows, for example, that the lowest sort, when speaking about etching, speak of Dürer. Where cinema is concerned, one usually shows one's refinement by inserting the good name of 'Grifschitz' [Griffith]—and so he talks about Stroheim. In the Hermitage he disregards Van Dyck, but extols Van Eyck. Da Vinci, of course, is fine, not for

'Gioconda', but for 'Madonna Litta', and so on. A very cultured young man. Today I'm going to introduce him to Japanese prints. I think he'll 'plunge'. But of course, the most unbearable of all are the musicians at the local restaurant! There're quite a few of them. Traditional to the point of indecency. They have a horrible trait: whenever they're not playing, they swarm all over the place. And everyone else suffers from this too . . .

I won't break down your staunch ideology of the working mass. Or else I'd tell you about the class hostility between us 'intelligentsia', and the aristocracy of the 'resort patients' and 'sanatoriumites'. Instead of high class books, there are 'health resort books' here. Whoever doesn't have them walks about slightly ashamed. Or about those who have to pay more for the very same thing. I'll also keep silent about our excursion on the Aphon. I'll simply say that 'it's wonderful there'. Numerous things of interest to see for 8 1/2 rubles there and back—I'll elaborate when I see you in person. I'm also stopping because in the beginning of your letter, you promised to write me the same amount in response. And I should spare your dear little hands and eyes in the name of new victories on the unacted front!

Farewell my beloved (Thierry-Sandre's *Beloved*, a novel translated from the French by M. E. Abkina, Kniga publishers, Moscow-Leningrad), till we meet again. Don't put on a wedding gown in the event of my death, for I'm quite devoted to you with all my soul.

S. Eisenstein

Usually during periods of 'my soul's depression', the tail of my straight and unbroken signature is embellished with a little cross. As you can see—the cross is slanted; perhaps that's a good sign of what I wish for you.

S.E.

Grisha naturally sends his greetings.

E to S

5 April 1929
Tselina Station

Esther!

Here you are:

I write to you, what
More can I say . . .

I can say that I don't want you to think any worse of me than you always do, for not coming to see you.

I'm writing you from the most far-flung outpost of Socialist Construction. From the 'Giant' State Farm. On the other side you'll see a few typical landscapes of this blessed region. It doesn't come across in the photo—it's too practical.

You now have an absolutely complete impression of our surroundings . . . (And, by the way, Happy Easter! Today's the first day of Easter.)

We're living at the above-mentioned private residence. The owner shares it with us.

The owner . . .

She makes ice-cream. Sells it at the market. Awful.

She makes kvass. Sells it at the market. Awful. (Judging by the sensation it evokes in the stomach, I believe this kvass has to be the ideal medium for corrosive etching.)

I think somewhere between the house and the cellar, she runs a secret public house. She has a daughter, Shurochka. Awful.

She keeps six women around her who are constantly scraping, splashing, cooking, frying and sizzling over the primus stove.

They are staunch believers in God.

That's a big advantage for us: we comb our hair in the icon-glass since there are no mirrors.

The climate is basically tropical.

There are animals here: cows (not many), horses (a lot), lizards (a lot of green and grey ones).

Tractors. Most of them are also green and grey. They make a deafening noise, but they're so far out in the field, you can't hear them. They plough and sow day and night (even though nights were created for wholly different entertainments. Incidentally, some of them are girls. Or rather, were—now they're tractor drivers). It's hard to tell them apart. They're just as sunburnt. Just as covered all over with oil—they also curse. Good girls.

It's wonderful to write to you. Like speaking into a well. Or like a dog: you pull me by the tail. I whine. But the opposite is not possible: in a day or two we move on from here.

More:

The Buddhists pray like this: they chew a little piece of paper and spit at the statue. If it sticks—that's good. If it doesn't stick—that's bad. And Buddha can't answer. In the present case, it's Buddha who's sending. I hope it sticks. And you can't answer. Eh! Eh! Eh!...

There's also a transporter here: 'Wheat'. That's her last name. Honest to God. And very knowledgeable about ethnography, flora and fauna. She sometimes gives us talks on the various religions of the region.

Imagine, what a culture!

For 25 versts around, not a single church!!!

The reason there're no churches is because everyone here is a member of a sect. Baptists, new-Israelites, Mormons, roamers, milkers, Khlysts.

Because of them, if you want to hear an Easter Service in a true Orthodox Church, you have to ride thirty versts on wretched horses.

Today, trains took away the tractors to other state farms. Lots of emotion.

We'll be filming a tractor parade for several days. And for the First of May, we've accepted the Armed Forces' invitation to the Parade in Rostov.

Comrade Kovtyukh's orders. He's the model for Kozhukh in *The Iron Stream*. The other officers are all cavalry heroes from Babel's *Red Cavalry*.

Babel told us about them.

'Wheat' approaches our window in a grey jacket . . .

Shurochka just brought back the empty ice-cream buckets from the market . . .

Our expedition has gone to the local shooting gallery.

I'm thinking about you.

. . . Outside the window, 'Wheat' is giving Shurochka a triple Easter kiss. They're exchanging 'pysanki' (that's those painted eggs) . . .

I'm thinking of you . . .

Write me without fail. Put it in an envelope and give it to me when I get there.

S. Eisenstein

P.S. In Rostov, I ran into Kopalin. Stepanov is here.* Almost died from inflammation of the lungs. He, not me. The devil only knows! There's no escape from *these* unacteds!!!

Grisha sends his greetings.

E to S, the first postcard from Europe

19 September 1929
Frankfurt

Well how about your 'SA' [the journal 'Soviet Architecture']! The architecture! Some very splendid people, Frankfurt architects, took us to see this curiosity and perversion of the principles of architecture. Truly functional forms and . . . a church. I'll write you from here so you can establish some contacts with the architects. We've spent some absolutely marvellous days here.

S. Eisenstein

* Ilya Kopalin and Vladimir Stepanov are documentary cameramen. Stepanov was then making a film of the 'Giant' State Farm.

S to E   4 November 1929
                                                    Alupka (in transit)

Dear Sergei Mikhailovich!

I send you October greetings. I very much want to hear about
you. How are you? What are your thoughts, plans? Did you
receive my letter?

Write to Tiflis, poste restante. I've long been meaning to
write you my thoughts on the period of the victory over un-
principledness. In *Old and New,* no one understood or recognized
its deep principledness.

I shake your hand in friendship.

                                                    E. Shub

E to S, a postcard   6 November 1929
                                                    London

Dear Esther Ilinishna!

We've now been a week in London. Of everything I've seen so
far, this city is certainly the most wonderful. I'm now writing
you from Parliament: MacDonald, Henderson, Baldwin have
already spoken. We're drinking tea and getting ready to
move on.

I'll write you a letter.

                                                    S. Eisenstein

E to S, a postcard   November 1929
                                                    Paris

Dear Esther Ilinishna!

Don't curse me for not writing. All these delays have caused
me a lot of pain. But at last we're in Paris. Greetings from the
paradise of lace. Greetings from [Hans] Richter. We've now
met 5 times!

Always yours

                                                    Eisenstein

E to S, a postcard   1930
                                                        La Sarraz

Dear Esther Ilinishna!

We send you our heartfelt greetings from this blessed spot, the
palace of Madame de Mandrot, where they play at Congress,
while we rest in the bosom of nature.

                                                        S. Eisenstein
                                                        G. Alexandrov

E to S   7 April 1930
                                                        Southampton

Dear Esther Ilinishna!

I've just stepped on deck for a two-week sail to New York,
and then—to Hollywood. It's all so strange. We waited for so
long, and then everything fell into place and was ready in
just 10 days.

I'm coming to my senses somewhat and will start writing.

Write me without fail. After all, you owe me!

Address: The Not-Unknown Film Centre Paramount—
Publix Corporation, to me.

I embrace you. Always yours

                                                        Eisenstein

E to S, a packet of postcards   29 May 1930
                                                        New York

1. Dear Esther Ilinishna!

There's absolutely no time to write! My eyes are dazzled;
these postcards are living proof of the reason why. The 'Estab-
lishment' where I'm working is the 'Board of Paramount'.

2. The tallest building (an even taller one is under construction).

3. The same building, hidden in clouds (not bad!).

Give my warmest regards to Anechka* and don't forget your sincerely devoted

Eisenstein

4. A view from the roof of this building in clear weather. NB (Statue of Liberty in the distance).

E to S   June 1930
                                              Hollywood

Dear Esther Ilinishna!

No time to write—so many things to do and impressions. But it's absolutely incomprehensible why you don't write. I keep au courant of the progress of your work (through Pera [Atta-sheva]), but only the general features; you could certainly write me about this and about yourself. And about me too . . . You know how much I value everything that you think about me.

Write.

Instead of words, I'm sending you a number of images—pictures are always more expressive than words!

I embrace you and urgently wait for letters about you, about cinema and about me!

Always yours

Eisenstein

S to E   2 August 1930
                                              Moscow

Dear Sergei Mikhailovich!

I'm at Pera's in order to write you briefly about myself. I've been working a lot the last few months. My picture, *Today*—

* Shub's daughter Anne.

4

both here and in America is in many ways, like the path of my
work—curious.* I know you would approve of much in it.
If it gets sent to 'Amtorg', I'll let you know. Try to see it and
show to Americans how Soviet eyes see the facts of American
life. GRK gave the picture First Category. But the fighting
continues—and not healthy—between the acteds and the
documentarists. I'm very weary. I'm leaving on the 5th for a
six-week rest. And now about you. This is extremely complicated. You've been living such a distant, almost alien life
for almost a year. What do I think of you? You are close and
dear to me, and I am worried for you in a complicated way,
a worry sometimes happy, sometimes complicated and con-
tradictory.

It's good to gallop around the world. To see so much as you
have in this short period—to see with your own eyes—to
control what you see with your brain. I know that this year
will enter into the years of your life to the advantage of your
intellectual growth. I know that the point is not the pictures
you made in Paris or will make in America (although that too
is also important for you in some ways). What's important is
how you'll return; what's important is what you'll want and
will do here.

And it's important that you did not spend this year here.

That you didn't live with what we lived. This year is remarkable in many ways—severe, difficult, but a fine Bolshevik
year. You've lived far away, as someone else—and I don't
know which would be more important for you, for your work:
Hollywood and those opportunities that are given you now,
or the area of complete collectivization here in 1930—with our
primitive, poor technology, a theme understood and formulated
in cinema by you, but not others, others, others.

Don't take everything I've written as the crude ecstasy of
an Intellectual. I don't know how to write. I love to talk with
you—and so, so much has happened this year. Or maybe we
experience time here in a different way.

But I am your friend. And I want to be proud of you; that's

* Shub's *Today* was shown in the United States as *Cannons or Tractors?*

why I'm not indifferent to what you'll now be doing over there. I wish it would be *The Glass House*, only a little different from the *Glass House of 1930* that we talked about.* No 'stars' and breaking in every way all the production traditions of Holly-wood. Don't seduce anyone—and don't seduce yourself.

Firmly, à la Eisenstein, and especially in this case, long live Cynicism—your cynicism! Please, give the Americans some-thing in the vein of *The Glass House*.

It was hard to begin. I'll write you often from now on. And you write. When I get back to Moscow I want to find an answer and a letter.

Don't forget me.

I wish you all the very best.

Your Esther Ilinishna

E to S   1930 [September/October?]
                                   Hollywood

Dear Esther Ilinishna!

I'm a pig—you probably haven't gotten used to that yet. You wrote me such a fine, wonderful letter (I could practically hear it, I'm so used to hearing you regularly on the telephone) and I still haven't written: but it's not from thoughtlessness, it's the opposite—I don't want to answer just 'any way', but there's absolutely no time to answer properly. We've worked intensively on the scenario for *An American Tragedy*—today we go to New York for a discussion with Dreiser. Write me what you think of this, but only after having precisely pictured to yourself how I would make it. You know me well enough for this.

Write.

With all my heart, your S.M.

* *The Glass House* was one of the first projects thought unsuitable for Paramount.

E to S   1930 [October?]
                                                  New York

Dear Esther Ilinishna!

This is the building they've just completed. It's so tall, that
from the seventy-first floor, it seems as though I can see you—
but it's an optical illusion . . . it's the Statue of Liberty.

For four days we raced here on an express from the opposite
coast, in order to definitely decide in a few days whether *An
American Tragedy* is to be or not to be. I think this will also
settle the problem of the duration of our stay here.

I'll write without fail as soon as anything definite is determined, but in the meantime I'm stuffing myself with Negro
impressions.

Always sincerely yours — S. Eisenstein

S to E   3 October 1930
                                                  Moscow

Dear Sergei Mikhailovich!

For two months I rested in the Caucasus. I hoped to find an
answer to my letter in Moscow. Instead of a letter, I received
your and Chaplin's photos. They made me very happy, but
your letter would have made me happier. I wanted to know
about you as much as possible directly from you.

From Pera I learned you have chosen Dreiser's novel, *An
American Tragedy*, to work on. I know this novel well. The
opportunity to depict the various social layers of America must
have interested you. I think so. But over it all there densely
hangs Dreiser's truth of life; for instance, the fate of the novel's
hero. There's no way you can get around that, no matter how
much mercy you have in Dreiser's lofty 'spirituality' and 'love
of mankind'.

From this comes the 4th–10th step of *A Woman of Paris*.
Don't get angry, dear. I think it's wonderful when you and

Chaplin regard each other lovingly (Chaplin is marvellous), but there are no intersections in your creative paths. You are a man of a different anger, a different lyricism, a different love than Chaplin. And I love your cynicism (you have another) when you wrap yourself in it, because of some complicated inner emotion, your utterly youthful romanticism in the serious and stern man of Soviet days.

I'm also not completely clear on what you're planning to do with sound for this theme. Are you able to imagine now the huge interest which grows with each day among broad Soviet strata towards America? It's significant that Ludwell Denny's book* had an absolutely exceptional success this year not only in readers' circles, but also in political ruling circles. I don't think there's any need to tell you what dictated this exceptional interest. Would *An American Tragedy* by Sergei Eisenstein be able to satisfy this interest? Think about this. Very, very much.

And also (although this is less important), have you considered the expectations, both friendly and unfriendly, which are being placed upon your American work? Forgive me for writing you about this without knowing all the compelling circumstances. That's your fault. I am deeply and as a friend touched by everything connected with you and your work. Perhaps I'm wrong. Everything is more clear to you over there. Have you thought about your treatment of *An American Tragedy*? There are, after all, very many curious possibilities for sound there as well. And then the New York citadel, as shot by you, I think would prove of enormous interest for Americans as well.

I await your letter. A lot will then become clearer and more defined to me.

The 'atmosphere' around you has completely cleared up. You have true friends here. We have no grudge. We're wait-

---

* One of Denny's two books on the 'petroleum wars', *We Fight for Oil* (1928), and *America Conquers Britain: a Record of Economic War*; the latter is the more likely reference as it was first published in February 1930, giving time for its success in Russian translation that Shub mentions.

ing for you calmly, patiently, but we're very much waiting
for you.

All the best.

Esther Shub

E to S, a fragment   Mexico

[. . .] Thinking in terms of cinema, I present you my closest
neighbour—a pyramid. Telotsotlan [?] in montage pieces from
long shot to close-up from four positions—that's the extent of
research into montage-thought in America. The ways of the
Lord are inscrutable . . . and so here I am in Mexico. I think
my leaving Hollywood was for the best; what could I do there!
Given the political circumstances that were created, it would
have been inconceivable to make anything with those people.
I'm now making a Mexican 'culture-film'—a travelogue. As
you can see, the specimens here are worthy of attention.

Flaherty got me interested in Mexico—and I him in the
Soviet Union. The old man (he's completely grey) got all
excited and went to visit his family for Christmas, fully determined to work in the Soviet Union on a series of ethnographic
films. He is remarkable and you will certainly love him. My
leave ends in February and I don't think I'll be very late—
except I might be delayed a bit if I go to Japan. Everything
here is remarkable and strong: the bull fights, which I've been
to, cockfights, and pagan Indian dances in honour of Catholic
saints. I think I'll travel over the whole country. [. . .]

E to S   4 July 1931
                Mexico

My dear friend Esther Ilinishna!

The colour of this paper is the degree of incandescence of my
feelings of friendship for you that rage unabated in my breast!

Pera's message, that you think I've struck you from my memory, overwhelmed me with grief. That is foolishly, utterly and totally false! I would have more grounds to be convinced of such a 'nothing-of-the-kind'—a lonely wanderer in a foreign land, forgotten by you and your letters.

We've been travelling up and down the whole map of Mexico. Pushkin himself wrote about us: 'they're washed by the rains, covered with dust'. The work is complicated, difficult, multi-lingual, but hellishly fascinating. I'm not thinking about the final results—after *General* [shown as *Old and New*], I consider myself incompetent to judge the qualities of my future productions. I didn't think I could go on living after its fate— but time heals all wounds, and perhaps the only trace left by it,—is the fact that I'm interested in everything besides . . . the cinema. Cinema is absorbing only in so far as it is 'a miniature experimental universe' by which one can study the laws of phenomena much more interesting and significant than fleeting little pictures; especially today with all its deafening noise or non-stop talk. Perhaps it's a very judicious period of 'cleansing', for the future cinema will need a complete overhaul, and there will be no rubble left of our dear deceased, responsible . . . works. The living ethnography that surrounds me is far more fascinating than any cinema and especially documentary. The change now going on in the audience psychology in the USSR is of colossal interest. I'm receiving very scanty information, but even so one can sense the most curious changes in the viewer's pulse. I'm even going to risk writing an article about it—for I think that half a world away, I'm better able to sense its beating. These changes lie not at all where our inveterate scribblers suggest! This is all written just for you—as though it were a telephone conversation, which, alas!, hasn't taken place for almost two years now.

What are you currently doing? What direction are you thinking in—are there also perspectives of colossal revision facing your line, but along the same tracks?

At times I'd like to work in the theatre. In a good one, a real one. So strong is my reaction to the cinema. Even though I've never worked so conscientiously as I am now here.

I'm no longer the slightest bit concerned with problems of montage. And, it's terrible to say, sound film even less. It's interesting, what kind of picture will come out of such conditions?! Maybe it'll prove to be exactly what's needed?! What a laugh that would be!

Mexico is astonishing, especially for me. Picture to yourself a country across which is stretched . . . my personality. You already know its diapason, from one ugly feature to another, and the contrast of all my passions and interests.

Well, I think I've stupefied you enough as punishment for your lack of faith in me.

I await your letters—soon and detailed, and I remain with all my soul.

Always yours

S. Eisenstein

See you soon!

S to E   9 September 1931
                                                Moscow

Dear Sergei Mikhailovich!

I've finally got around to writing you. Very complicated and troubled the days pass and there are few hours of quiet. I often think about you, about your work, about your return, about the position and life you'll find for yourself here. I'm glad that you'll soon be in Moscow, and most of all I fear delays. You need to return as soon as absolutely possible to the USSR. That's why I'm writing you first and, knowing my love and friendship, you will understand how thoroughly and carefully I've thought this over. I know you've had many difficulties with your Mexican work; I know you're carried away with it, that probably a whole number of your aims take on a special sharpness in the process of realizing them in material that is completely new for you. I understand all this very well, but I feel even more strongly, and I still say—you must return as soon as possible. I know how you gathered material for the *Battleship*, I know the paths and cross-roads of *October* and *General Line*, I know your special approach which distinguishes you from everyone else, of not being a slave to your initial script outlines, of understanding and listening to material during its conceptual and shooting stages and of moulding it to yourself, subjecting it to a new idea which arises in the process of work.

Dear, don't get angry at me for daring to assert across the ocean that the material you've already shot is completely sufficient for your new work. I saw all your photos at Pera's. The first time I kept expecting shots connected with my conceptions of Mexico. From everything I know about it, what most stuck in my memory and entered my consciousness was 'Revolutionary Mexico' by the remarkable John Reed. But then I understood and became very interested in what you are doing. I think it's all correct and very interesting. I think that your Mexico will be a revelation and a revolutionary revelation. I'd like to explain very concisely and totally why I am hurrying you and so insistently asking you to return. It's not possible to write truthfully about this. We need to talk, to understand each other completely, we need to overcome and strike out these enormous two years that have separated us; and yet for some reason I impertinently believe that even at a distance I know how you are and what makes up an intellectual day in your excessively expanding brain. And that's what makes you unique.

A small, leading group of film directors, fellow-travellers and Trade Unionists (I don't know about you, but these terms wrack me with pain), hemmed in by the grandiose events of the last few years, have finally decided to re-organize themselves from within, to organically link their creative thoughts with the tasks and goals of the country of Socialist Construction. [last page missing].

E to S, a fragment   28 March 1932

[. . .] We're doing four-hundred to five-hundred kilometres a day, racing across the most interesting part of America— the Negro States. An automobile gives us the chance to take our time and acquaint ourselves with everything worthy of attention,—and there's so much! Soon now we'll see each other and I'll tell you all about it in much more colourful words . . . I gave a lecture at a Negro University today in . . . Charleston (yes, yes, the same city the dance comes from). I gave a talk on the Soviet Union (partially about family life, abortion and similar questions) in . . . a black Baptist church! (on Easter Sunday). Tomorrow we'll be in Washington. And then New York. [. . .]

S to E, on his 36th birthday   23 January 1934
                                             Moscow

Dear friend!

Today is a truly festive day for me, and considering my spiritual gloom, that should tell you more than any words could how dear you are to me, and how glad I am that you're living in our great world.

May the day when you'll say 'My plans are choking me' not come soon—*fantastically* not soon.

You will have *three lives.*

Live long.

Live eternally.

I kiss you.

                                                   Esther

S to E and Attasheva   5 October 1934
                                            Smyrna, Turkey

My dear, ardent friends!

I very much wanted to write you together. The 21st, I left for
Smyrna. We took the Bosphorus route—the Marble Sea,
Dardanelles, the Aegean Sea. We travelled past the Lesbos
Islands—past Troy. We were shown Smyrna and its environs
by the governor of Smyrna. Ask Zarkhi to tell you about him
and you'll understand the whole colourfulness of this trip.

For four days I shot the Pergamon ruins and absolutely lost
my head. In spite of the terrible heat, working in the mountains,
all the various difficulties, I was happy to see the ruins pre-
served for thousands of years, towns of incomprehensible
beauty: temples, urban planning, halls, theatres, the circus,
gymnastic halls, the baths, statues, pillars, fortresses, towers—
it's all the result of cyclopean labour and on everything there
is the imprint of genius and beauty—it is great art. A theatre
for 15 thousand spectators, an amphitheatre situated with its
base at the foot of a great mountain. All around is a chain of
mountains—sitting at the very top, one can distinctly hear the
voices coming up from the stage. At the foot of the stage is the
white, marble temple of Dionysus. In the temple of Dionysus,
I discovered plumbing. I thought of you, dear Sergei Mikhailovich. I wanted to hear you telling me about the kinds of
spectacles that took place in such theatres. A few days ago,
we went to some place, God only knows where, in the mountains. There, in the mountains, on the shores of a mountain
lake, I shot the dances of the Zebecs. As you can see, I'm
travelling quite a bit, I'm seeing a lot that's interesting, but
I'm not completely satisfied, because I see all too well that a
great work is not to be had—the 'boss' is loathsome. He himself
doesn't know what he wants. A crafty, mean, tasteless, petty
tyrant. He's mean. He's arranging his political and financial
affairs. I'm afraid my endurance will not hold out for long.
I'll edit Pergamon for him and Smyrna and I'll take off. I very
much want to shoot Istanbul. It could be done so interestingly,

but I'm sure that it won't happen. For personal reasons, the boss is least interested in Istanbul. There's a lot I can't write you about in a letter.

I'm sunburnt, bitten badly all over by midges, my lips are blistered from the sun and I'm exhausted.

I want very much to hear about you, dear. How about the theatre, are you working yet? How's the book? How's your mood? Write about yourself and don't forget me.

Pera, I won't tell you what to write about—you already know. You know how much I need your letters, my dear friend.

Tomorrow I'll start filming Smyrna. I'm leaving from here for Istanbul the 15th–16th of October. Write to Istanbul. I'll be living there at our Embassy. You have the address.

I kiss both of you—each separately and together.

Your Esther

Greetings to Zarkhi, Olga Viktorovna [Tretyakova] and the others.

S to E, on location   1935 [November?]
                                         Moscow

Dear Sergei Mikhailovich!

I've waited and waited for the letter you promised, but you're silent. Such is woman's lot: whomever we love, we 'indulge'. So I'm writing you. The 'events and happenings' that occurred during your absence were not so many,—but there were some, nonetheless. I'll tell you about them—maybe it will entertain you.

First of all—*Aerograd.*

As you know, the press acclaimed it. Now, my opinion—perhaps it will interest you: I consider *Aerograd* a significant thing, a phenomenon of art, and very Dovzhenkian. I'm very anxious to hear your word. I don't want to write about *Aerograd* in great detail. Let's talk about it in person. Ehrenburg was shown your [*Bezhin Meadow*] fragments. I don't know which ones. I don't think it should have been done without you. He is delighted with the material, the young boy, but he very much dislikes Orlov[?] and Rzheshevsky's dialogue. I think a lot of what he said to me is worth considering. But I want to discuss this with you in person. I so passionately wish you success in your work, that I react to everything concerning it with a personal bias. May I? Both *Aerograd* and many other things that I've had to think about in the last few weeks (and especially the Stakhanov rally, which it turned out after all I was able to attend) have led me to quite a few conclusions. It's all directly connected with thoughts about your work. But this too I want to discuss with you, because in person you forgive my confused articulation and always perceive the main thing that excites me and what it is I want to convey to you. See what a long conversation you're in for!

I've kept one story for you. It will give you pleasure. It's depressing to write about myself ... But I'm calm because I *know*, as never before, that I've started to understand a lot of things better, that I've become *wiser*, and most important, that my mind and eyes have not betrayed me and that I'm always ready for work.

I kiss you.

Your Esther

When will you be coming?

Send me at least a telegram so that I'll know you have not altogether forgotten me.

S to E   25 August 1938
                                           Moscow

'Everything that exceeds the limits of the ordinary, receives the most foolish interpretation, for to one's taste is repellent both that which is above it and beneath it' (Montaigne).

Dear Old Man! I wish you everything wonderful that 'exceeds the limits of the ordinary'.

E. Shub
The Summer of 'Alexander Nevsky'

E to S

27 March 1939
Moscow

Be sure to read my scenario [*Ferghana Canal?*] today. With absolute attentiveness. And be sure to bring it to me tomorrow at the studio.

I eagerly await your opinion.

The Old Man

S to E, on location

6 October 1939
Moscow

Dear Old Man! I got back yesterday from Kislovodsk. I rested, got better and am calm now. Pera is still in Kislovodsk. Poor thing, she still is very sick. Frequent headaches and nausea. Her concussion was apparently serious.

I still haven't seen any Moscovites yet. Moscow right now is quite special.

How are you? How's the work? When should we expect you? Rumour has it that the footage you've sent is extremely interesting. I'm glad.

Write me about yourself. I've missed you very much. There's a lot I want to tell you.

Greetings to Eduard—my very warmest.

I'll write you in more detail in a few days about Moscow and Moscovites.

I embrace and kiss you.

Esther

E to S

December 1939
Moscow

My dear, ardent friend Esther!

As you pointed out, I haven't written you all this time. I haven't felt like writing or even living. I've wanted to just be, like grass, and grass doesn't write letters. I'd just started to come out of it. And again the Mexican affair, with all its vileness, whirls everything all to hell. What bastards they are who are responsible for all this!

I received your kind letter and was deeply touched by it. Essentially I'm afraid to think about the questions you touched on: but maybe it's all over? For the last two days, another monstrous spell of depression. I'll hardly see the sun in diamonds . . .

I want to go to Persia.

Perhaps that would compensate somewhat for my open wounds.

I'm holding myself on brakes: I'm afraid to go out—I may not restrain myself.

Don't pay much attention—perhaps it's a whim . . . And anyway it's swinish of me to write you about this. Your own chickens aren't pecking either!

I'm waiting for a letter from you (this time in your own hand and not that of . . . Fadeev, as in the first letter. Although I was cheered and very touched by it).

I warmly, warmly embrace you, dear Esther.

Your unhappy brother

S. Eisenstein

S to E, in Alma-Ata

1942
Moscow

Dear Sergei Mikhailovich!

I send you warm greetings. If you only knew, dear, how far away you're living.

It's frightening here. Moscow is a war-time city and is living in war. I recall the Alma-Ata heat like a dream and the provincial, measured, quiet life of the inhabitants of the 'Laureate'.

I'm working a lot and it's difficult. I rotate round and round all day between Potylikha, the Newsreel Studio, and the [Film] Committee. Potylikha is overgrown with grass and tall weeds. Total silence.

It's depressing to the point of pain.

I've seen Ehrenburg, Fadeev, Solntseva's here, Agapov— they all had a lot of news, but you didn't write me anything about them. Pera is putting together an American festival to which they're planning to invite you and Kozintsev. Will you come? In my opinion, it would be worth it.

I see Pera often—greetings to Magarill and Kozintsev, and Marina Ladynina and Raizman.

I kiss you.

Esther

How are you taking care of my property?

S to E, in Alma-Ata

1944 [August?]
Moscow

Dear Sergei Mikhailovich!

Have you come any closer to Moscow in all this time? You're very much missed here. And you need to be here. To live and to work, in spite of the many difficulties, you'd be better off here than in Alma-Ata. All the news of the Film Committee, Comrade Polonsky has already told you. Both Vishnevsky and Dovzhenko asked a lot about you and are interested. Your film [*Ivan Grozny*] has practically become a legend. So hold on and descend like a thunderbolt in a flash of lightning. Like Jupiter. Pera is very busy with the anniversary edition of '25 Years of Soviet Cinema'. At Narkomindel and VOKS there

are receptions—I'm sorry that you're not among the guests.
Don't forget me.

Esther. Write.

S to E, at the Kremlin Hospital   1946 [February?]
                                                 Moscow

Dear Sergei Mikhailovich, my dearest friend!

When I came home I learned what had happened to you. I'm
very grieved. I know you're better and that you'll soon be
completely well. You can and must be completely healthy.
You must organize your life so that not the slightest trace of
what happened will ever occur again.

From all sides I'm told that the colour episode of *Ivan*
produces just as stunning an impression as *Potemkin* did in its
time, and the rest is very much acclaimed.

I'll have my leg in a plaster cast till the 7th of March; the
pain is still strong, and I have to lie down. My telephone
number is: G 1-14-75.

When you're able to, call me. I'm thinking about you a lot.
For the last two months I've been thinking a lot about illness.
There was time and pain enough to do so. So that's what I
thought about. I wish you only the best, but most of all,
health, complete good health.

I kiss you.

Esther

E to S   1946
                                                 Moscow

Dear Esther!

Your note made me very happy. On the 2nd of February, I
made the final 'cuts' on the picture, raced over to the Dom

Kino and suggested that the next day I would begin fulfilling all my moral obligations—the first of which was to visit you in the hospital, which I hadn't been able to do earlier. And then: almost a 'beautiful death' in the embraces of Circe . . . But I somehow managed to emerge and it seems I'm even getting better. However, for two weeks I haven't even been able to sit up. As soon as they allow me to get near a telephone, I'll call you at once.

Get better!

I warmly embrace you.

Greetings.

S. Eisenstein

An Application from Samuel Beckett

Why It Didn't Happen

Beckett's letter would certainly have attracted Eisenstein's attention—and action—if it had not arrived in the last half of 1936.

That was a year that turned bad for Eisenstein. Most of *Bezhin Meadow* had been shot when he and the production were stopped by smallpox.

The forced interval grew more fatal as it grew longer. Even before the smallpox there had been official doubts—'Isn't the imagery getting too biblical?' 'Why does the Father look and behave like Pan?' While still in his quarantine hut, Eisenstein began to sketch modifications in structure and 'story' and by the time work was again possible, he invited Babel to collaborate with him on a drastically revised script that would answer his own doubts as well as those from above.

Beckett's application was lost in the shuffle.